OXFORD
PRIMARY
art

Transport and journeys

Norman Binch

Maps

Early maps were inaccurate compared with today's map records. They were often attractively illustrated and decorative.

The map of Saxon London is quite plain, simply showing the area and main routes for travellers. The map of Venice is made to look as if it's modelled, like an aerial view of the city.

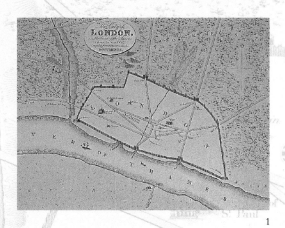

1

2

Marco Polo's account of Asia is more of an illustration of his journeys than a map.

What information can you get from these maps?

1. London in Saxon times

2. Map of Venice. From the gallery of maps

3. Marco Polo's account of the map of Asia

Working horses

Until the invention of the motor car and lorry, horses and other strong animals were used for travel and for heavy work. Horses were specially bred. What they were used for affected the way they looked, just like the difference between a mountain bike and a racing bike.

What are the differences between these horses and the horses on page 6/7?

1

2

Leonardo da Vinci, as well as being a successful artist was also
a scientist, an inventor, a musician and poet. These are some
drawings of ideas for war machines.

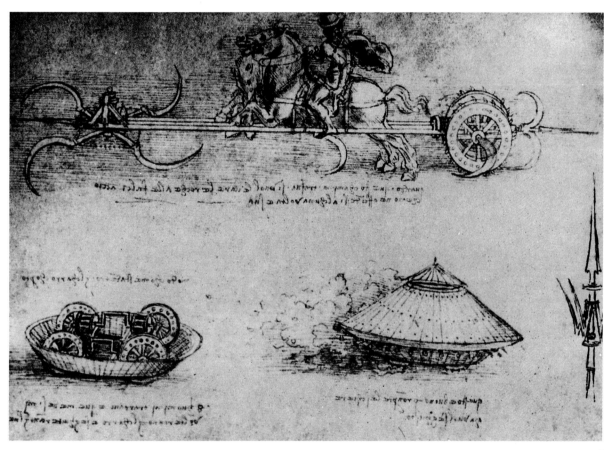

3

Travelling on horseback

These paintings are of people using horses to travel. Each is painted in a different style.

Toulouse-Lautrec has used watercolour to make this sketch of 'A Ride in the Country' and captures the feeling of a Sunday afternoon outing.

Raoul Dufy also uses watercolour but he uses it very loosely to create an impression of movement, light and colour.

1

2

Mantegna, who painted this horse nearly 500 years ago, was interested in *perspective*. He wanted to paint the horse from a three-quarter frontal view. If you try to do the same you'll find how difficult it is.

3

1. Henri de Toulouse-Lautrec (1864-1901). A Drive in the Country

2. Raoul Dufy (1877-1953). The Kessler Family on Horseback, 1931

3. Andrea Mantegna (1431-1506). From the wallpainting in the Camera degli Sposi, Palazzo Ducale, Mantua

Boats

Boats can be very simple and made by hand, like the basketry coracle, or they can be highly complicated like the early steamboat. The way a boat looks is related to what it is used for and how it is made.

Why do you think the boat from Kashmir looks like this?

How do you think each of these boats was propelled through the water?

1

2

佃
沖
晴
天
の
不
二

1. **Basketry coracle from the Philippines**

2. **Boat on Dal Lake, Kashmir**

3. **Kuyinyoshi (1797-1861). Mount Fuji from Tsukuda - Oki, with fishing nets**

4. **J.V. Cornell. Steamboat 'Iron Witch' c. 1846**

3

IRON WITCH.

4

Model boats

These are models of boats made by craftspeople for different reasons. Sam Smith was a toy-maker but also made models like this which 'worked'. Models like this are called *automata*: they have moving parts.

1. Sam Smith. Boat

2 and 3. Sam Smith. Boat. Details

4. Nathan Ward. Shelf piece, 1990

Nathan Ward's 'Shelf piece' is a boat made from carved wood, hammered metal and scrap materials. He is interested in the general idea of journeys and voyages.

Can you imagine what this piece might be about? You could try making something to express the idea of a sea journey yourself.

4

Shipwrecks

Shipwrecks are dramatic subjects for artists to paint.

Winslow Homer's watercolour is about a ship wrecked in a hurricane.

Can you guess the story behind the picture?

'The Raft of the Medusa' is a famous painting by Géricault. It tells the story of the passengers from a sunken ship who were cast adrift on a raft. They suffered terribly, and many died, until the survivors saw a ship and were rescued.

All of the figures in the *composition* were drawn from real life. Géricault even drew dead and dying people. He made many studies before deciding on his final painting.

1

2

3

1. Winslow Homer (1836-1910).
After the hurricane

2. Théodore Géricault (1791-
1824). Study for the Raft of the
Medusa

3. Théodore Géricault. Pen and
ink study for the Raft of the
Medusa, 1817

Canals and rivers

Rivers, canals, barges and boats make interesting subjects. The shapes of boats are pleasing and there are reflections, light and colour in busy scenes on the water.

The styles of the paintings are different from each other. Can you describe the differences?

Why do you think the shapes of boats are usually so pleasing?

1. Margaret Loxton. Limehouse Basin, Regents Canal, London

2. Claude Monet (1845-1926) Bathers at La Grenouillière, 1869

3. André Derain (1880-1954). Barges on the Thames

4. Margaret Loxton. Narrow boats

4

Cars and buses

Dame Laura Knight has painted a scene from
the races at Epsom. Can you see how she has
created the feeling of a grey day? Looking at
the design of the cars, can you guess roughly
when the painting was done?

1. Dame Laura Knight (1877-1970). A grey day at Epsom

2. Painted clay chivas (local buses). Sandez Sisters workshop, Colombia

3. Allen Jones. Bus II, 1962

These local buses are part of a long tradition of making models of everyday things in Colombia. Look how carefully the details are modelled.

Allen Jones has made his bus almost abstract. He has created a new image based on the colours and shapes of a bus.

2

3

Decorated cars

In recent years the BMW car manufacturer in Germany has commissioned artists from different parts of the world to paint a car in their own style.

These two examples show how traditional styles of painting from Africa and Australia can be used to decorate a car.

Can you think of other traditional styles which would be good to use? You could try decorating a model of a car to see how it would look.

1

2

3

1. Esther Mahlangu at work on the BMW

2. A decorated BMW. Ndebele Art

3. Michael Jagamara Nelson working on the BMW

4. Decorated BMW. Papunya painting - aerial views of the landscape. Aboriginal Art

4

Flight

The first flight ever made was in a hot air balloon but it caught fire. This drawing shows the design of a balloon which was filled with Hydrogen. Do you know why these balloons fly?

Hang-gliders are a common sight today. Can you say how this early design is different from modern ones?

This is a technical illustration of Concorde which shows you all the compartments and working parts.

The British Airways Trident was one of the most successful passenger aircraft. Compare its shape with Concorde.

1. First flight in a hydrogen balloon, 1783. Jack Charles and Noel Robert

2. Early hang-glider. Otto Lilliental

3. Technical Illustration of Concorde

4. Hawker-Siddeley Trident IE

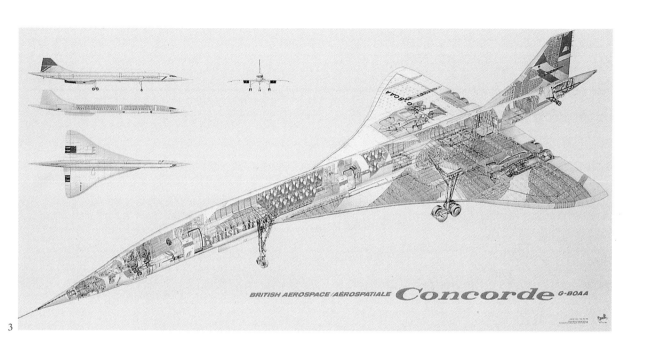

3

BRITISH AEROSPACE/AÉROSPATIALE *Concorde* G-BOAA

Space flight and model aeroplanes

This space capsule flies in space but doesn't look anything like an aeroplane. Do you know why? Think of the difference between *designing* for space flight compared with designing aeroplanes for everyday use.

1

Ann Carrington enjoys making these large models of early aeroplanes out of scrap materials, such as tin cans, bowls and cooking pans. You could try making your own models out of scrap.

1. Apollo 10 Command Module which carried three astronauts around the Moon in May 1969

2. Ann Carrington. Models of aeroplanes made from scrap

2

Kite flying

Steve Brockett does workshops with schools, helping children to make exciting kites.

Simple kites are fairly easy to make and to fly. More complicated kites can be made to do aerobatics. These kites are made as an art form and are meant to be beautiful and decorative. They look just as good when they aren't flying.

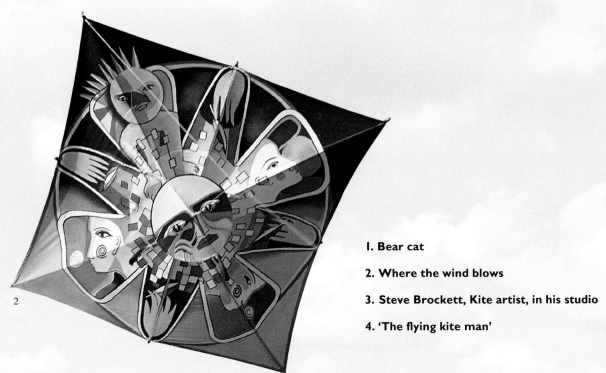

1. Bear cat

2. Where the wind blows

3. Steve Brockett, Kite artist, in his studio

4. 'The flying kite man'

3

4

Trains

These two early trains show how quickly design improvements can be made. There were only five years between them yet the Tank locomotive looks much more advanced. Compare them with the design for the modern train. What are the main differences?

1

2

1. Passenger locomotive, 1845 (model)

2. Tank locomotive, Dublin and Kingstown Railway, 1851

3. Sundberg and Ferar. Design for train, 1965. San Francisco Bay Area Rapid Transport system (BART)

4. Claude Monet (1840-1926). The Gare Saint-Lazare, 1877

3

When Monet painted this picture of the Gare Saint-Lazare station he was interested in the changing effects of light at different times of day. He also tried to capture the atmosphere of the railway station. Can you see how he has created these impressions?

4

Design now

These two designs are very new. The motorcycle is a *prototype* – a working model which can be tested before making them for sale.

The BMW model was made to try out different styles for a possible future production car

1. **Philippe Starck. Design for a motorcycle 1993**

2. **A Future BMW? Study prototype 1991**

3. **The 'Lotus Sport' racing bicycle. 1992**

1

2

The 'Lotus Sport' racing bicycle was ridden to a gold medal in the Barcelona Olympics.

What do all three designs have in common?

What do you imagine cars, cycles and motorcycles might look like in the future?

3

Things to do

Compare different maps of the same area, including some old ones, and look at the differences. Try making your own maps and illustrating them. Make some maps of walks in your area.

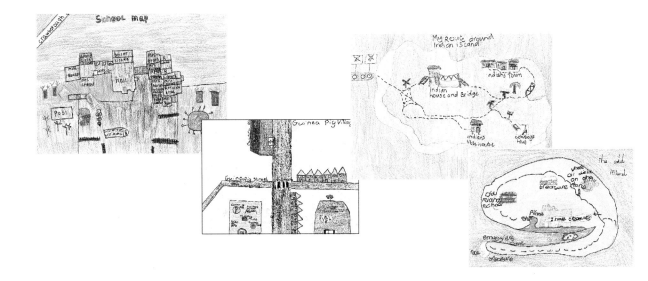

Make drawings and models of small boats. Design a boat for some purpose of your own - like a boat to take you and your friends on a holiday.

Try making models of the kind of transport you see every day.
Design transport for some purpose of your own – you can really
use your imagination for this!

What might it look like in the future?

Try to design other forms of transport which might be
used in the future.

Words to remember

automata – the name given to crafts pieces which 'work' or have moving parts – like a head with a mouth that opens and shuts.

composition – an arrangement of different things, like lines, shapes and colours to make an image.

designing – thinking, drawing and modelling to make new things or to improve the ones you have.

perspective – a way of drawing which helps you to represent what you can see from a particular viewpoint.

prototype – a working model which can be used for testing before making it in quantity.

style – the appearance of something – the way it looks which makes it different from others of the same kind – like different styles in the things you wear.

The publishers would like to thank the following for permission to reproduce photographs and other copyright material :

pp 2/3 *1 Bridgeman Art Library/Guildhall Library, London; 2 Bridgeman Art Library/Museo Correr, Venice. K & B News Foto, Florence; 3 Bridgeman Art Library/British Library, London;* **pp 4/5** *1 Tate Gallery; 2 Bridgeman Art Library/John Noott Galleries, Broadway, Worcs; 3* **pp 6/7** *1 Albi Museum; 2 Tate Gallery © DACS 1994; 3 Scala;* **pp 8/9** *1 Oxfam/Mike Wells; 2 Mustapha Salmi; 3 Victoria and Albert Museum; 4 Bridgeman Art Library/New York Historical Society;* **pp 10/11** *1 Crafts Council; 2 Crafts Council; 3 Crafts Council; 4 Crafts Council;* **pp 12/13** *1 Art Institute of Chicago; 2 Bridgeman Art Library/Christie's, London; 3 Bridgeman Art Library/Louvre, Paris ;* **pp 14/15** *1 Bridgeman Art Library/Private Collection; 2 National Gallery; 3 Bridgeman Art Library/City Art Gallery, Leeds © ADAGP, Paris and DACS, London 1994; 4 Bridgeman Art Library/Private Collection;* **pp 16/17** *1 Bridgeman Art Library/Christie's, London © The Estate of Dame Laura Knight, reproduced by*

permission of the Curtis Brown Group Ltd, London; 2 Oxfam/Letts; 3 Grenada Television; **pp 18/19** *1 BMW Munich; 2 BMW Munich; 3 BMW Munich; 4,BMW Munich;* **pp 20/21** *1 Science Museum; 2 Science Museum; 3 Science Museum; 4 Science Museum;* **pp 22/23** *1 Science Museum; 2 The artist;* **pp 24/25** *1 The artist;* **pp 26/27** *1 Science Museum; 2 Science Museum; 4 National Gallery;* **pp 28/29** *1 Design Museum; 2 BMW Munich; 3 Group Lotus Ltd*

We would also like to thank **Jeff Tearle** and the pupils of **Frideswide Middle School**, **Oxford**, and **Michael Mayell** and pupils of **St. Philip** and **St. James First School**, **Oxford**, for help with the Things To Do Sections. The photography in the Things To Do Sections was by **Martin Sookias** and **Mike Dudley**.